I WAS ARRESTED

A Candid Memoir of One
Cardiac Arrest Survivor

KOREY LOUGHRY

CONTENTS

Page

Introduction..1

Ch. 1 - Arrested 3

Ch. 2 - Heartfelt Gratitude 15

Ch. 3 - Continuing Kindness......................................27

Ch. 4 - Getting the Word Out.....................................33

Ch. 5 - Recovery Updates 37

Ch. 6 - Recovery Adjustments 57

Ch. 7 - Cause(s) 73

Ch. 8 - Hereafter...79

INTRODUCTION

Allow me to introduce myself. My name is Korey Loughry and I am a grateful survivor of cardiac arrest. This is a candid memoir of my recent journey.

I want to be clear from the outset that what I'm about to share with you is not the experience of *every* person who suffers cardiac arrest. And I don't say that just because 95% of people who experience cardiac arrest in the United States do not survive. Even of the 5% who *do* survive, each story is unique. What I'm sharing here is just one man's story.

What lies ahead is a detailed account of what happened on the day that my heart seized, quite unexpectedly. After that, I'll take you with me through the first six months of recovery that followed. My sincere desire is that, as you walk with me through these events, you would connect with some meaningful moments that might perhaps arrest *your own* heart. (Oh, wait… Well, you know what I mean.)

As I said, I've written this as a memoir, but I also wrote it to help educate. Having no medical background myself, there were a lot of terms I had to become familiar with. My first lesson was on the difference between *heart attack* and *cardiac arrest*. I had always assumed that they were synonymous terms, but I came to find out that while a heart attack occurs when the circulation of blood to the heart is disrupted by clogged arteries, cardiac arrest is an *electrical* issue where the heart stops beating altogether. I was surprised to learn that cardiac arrest can actually occur for reasons besides a heart attack. Throughout this experience, I also got to learn about things like: defibrillation, catheterization, stents, cardiac rehabilitation, cardiovascular disease, cardiovascular psychophysiology, and more.

But knowledge only goes so far, doesn't it? My greater hope is that, by reading this book, you'll not only become better *informed* (if you need that like I did), but that you might also be *inspired* to equip yourself with life-saving skills. Perhaps you could learn heart attack warning signs. Maybe you could become confident in using an AED (Automated External Defibrillator) or even able to perform CPR (Cardiopulmonary Resuscitation).

Whatever action you take—from whatever inspiration this little book may offer—I want to thank you from the bottom of my heart for taking the time to read it. And incidentally, the bottom of the heart is made up of two chambers known as the right and left ventricle. (Sorry. I'll try to keep my humor in check from now on.)

Korey Loughry

ARRESTED

1

On Nov. 28th, 2022, I posted the following on social media:

I Was Arrested

Almost a week ago, on Tuesday, November 22nd, I was arrested, which was a bummer, because the day started off so nice. I had been able to grind some stumps in Streetsboro for a friend that morning, and by a little after 11:00 I was headed back home to Kent to get a few things done around the house. About half way home, I started to realize this might not be such a "nice" day after all.

What I first noticed was that pain had begun to radiate out from the dead center of my chest over my sternum. As I tried to self-assess, I recalled that I had steak leftovers that morning, and figured this was just a really strong bout of indigestion that had suddenly come on, nothing more. I knew it couldn't be a heart attack, because, based on my vast knowledge of human anatomy (that's sarcasm), I knew that the heart is not "dead center," so no worries there.

As I stopped to put some air in my trailer tire (which naturally took longer than expected), I found myself wondering if that had been a bad decision. With the tire full, I got back in my truck and headed home. Within just a couple of minutes, my expectations about what was happening to me evolved, and I was compelled to text the sign-language emoji for "I love you" to my family, just in case. If this was going to be a heart attack, and that attack were to prove fatal, I didn't want to leave without letting Molly, Nathan and Kaylie know how much I love them, one last time.

As I got to the house, I can only describe the pain as raging. Foolishly, I opted to unhitch the trailer in its normal parking spot on the other side of our road. I recall being acutely aware that each of the half dozen or so steps of the unhitching process seemed to correspond with increasing intensity of that pain in the center of my chest. To keep my string of foolish decisions going, I then opted to drive the truck across the street to my parking spot next to the house.

Finally, at this point, I came to my senses and aimed for nothing else but getting inside and seeing if I could relieve my pain. I adjusted my belt, hoping for a little relief, entered the house, and immediately laid down on the floor just inside the door. It just felt like the right thing to do. On the one hand I was hoping that I could stretch out and relieve some internal pressure. But on the other hand I was resigned to the fact that—if this was something more serious—I would prefer to pass from this life quickly and quietly, content to go home to be with the Lord.

I laid there on the cool, hard floor thinking for a minute. It was painful to move, but perhaps foolish to not move. I suddenly remembered that I could check my blood pressure and perhaps differentiate indigestion from a heart attack. The blood pressure cuff was close by so I began the process. A minute or two passed as the blood pressure machine did its job. The results came but they weren't alarming one way or the other, because (to my embarrassment) I honestly couldn't recall what exactly *were* good or bad results. I decided that maybe I should search online for "heart attack symptoms."

The search results were crystal clear and I immediately dialed 911. The operator was efficient with her questions and then asked me if I wanted her to stay on the line until the paramedics arrived. By this point, merely answering that one question felt much too painful, so I ignored her, but she kindly did stay on the line.

Living so close to the Kent Fire Department, the squad was there within five minutes. They seemed to enter my dire need with great intention, and their excellent training was evident each step of the way as they quickly prepped me and got me into the ambulance. We headed out, sirens blaring.

Having grown up in this area, I knew exactly where the hospital was, and I knew how long it typically takes my non-emergency vehicle to get there. I expected it to take significantly less time today of course, but, as I lay there, I was getting increasingly anxious to arrive. I looked out the back of the ambulance to note that we were approximately halfway there, with no more than ten minutes to go.

The *next* thing I recall noting was that I must have fallen asleep because I woke up with an almost inebriating sense of euphoria coupled with a terrifying sense of confusion about what I was seeing. You see, the world around me took on not one layer of reality, but two. The ceiling of the ambulance, the paramedics—everything had a surreal double-layered quality to it. As someone who is very rational, I just wanted to make sense of it. And more than that, I really wanted it to go away quickly, but it wouldn't. It did go away, but only after

I woke up again, this time, as best as I could tell, inside the hospital. I could tell I had lost consciousness for a significant amount of time.

As I found myself conscious again, inside the hospital, I became instantly aware of an incredible flurry of activity—men and women racing to attach me to things, communicating instructions, and then transferring me from one surface to another. I was finally sure that I was indeed inside the hospital, and I was still alive. Questions and instructions came at me. Positive reassurances (that I felt I couldn't fully trust) did too. Then clarifications about where I was and what was being done to me, provided the first real measure of conscious comfort which, by this time, I really needed.

Some indistinguishable amount of time later, while still laying on the table in what I would later come to learn was "the Cath Lab," I felt, without warning, an incredible shock through my entire body. For some reason, it took me back to the sensation of the electric fences around the fields at the ranch I had worked at as a teenager. (As teenagers, we would, of course, sometimes fool around and grab the fence. Other times we would be surprised by it hitting our backs as we attempted to crawl under it.) But *this* shock seemed to be significantly stronger than the electric fences, on some incredible order of magnitude I found myself trying to calculate. I recall wondering if it wasn't too dissimilar to being executed in the electric chair, but with whatever amps/volts/or whatever, difference so that it didn't end a life, but rather save it. What I can say is that the pain was almost unbelievable, and witnessing my arms, legs, and head thrust into the air in an absolute instant, was something I'll never forget.

Being alert now, I could quickly tell that the caring and deliberate doctor was doing her work with such diligence. I felt I could trust her, but survival was still far from certain. I recall that she did "yell" at me a little, but I was just so sure we were just having a disagreement about what constituted my arm being in fact, "down." Under the circumstances, I was pretty sure that her opinion was probably the correct one, so I tried to be as cooperative as I could be in the midst of my confused stupor. She continued her remarkable work on my arteries until a genuine calm seemed to permeate the room. (Or perhaps it just permeated me.) I was then taken to a room to recover.

So, as you see, this "nice" day, ended up being life-altering. In the course of about an hour, I was later informed, I had experienced cardiac arrest (or to put it in more stark terms, "clinical death") four times. My left anterior descending artery had blocked 100% due to plaque that had "erupted", I was told. The experience of clinical death, as well as the subsequent life-saving defibrillation and CPR, each of the four times, took its toll *physically*, but the entirety of the experience took its toll on my *mind*, which is also healing, as intended.

   I wanted to write this all out, in part to help me process what all happened, but primarily because I so wanted to pay my sincere and heartfelt tribute to those tremendous people serving our community in such profound ways, beginning with the 911 operators who serve as that all-important first bridge connecting those in need with those who can help. Secondly I'm so deeply grateful to the first responders—in my case, the outstanding paramedic team from the Kent Fire Department whose caring, rapid, and skilled response saved my life. (I'm not sure I'll ever hear a siren again without praying for the squad and for those they are attempting to assist.) I want to express my immense gratitude to the Cardiac care team at UH Portage Medical, led by the remarkably kind and talented Dr. Myttle Mayuga who oversaw everything in the Cardiac Catheterization Lab, implanted the two stents that are allowing my blood to flow, and under whose care I will continue for some time ahead. And finally, I want to express my sincere gratitude to the Intensive Care Unit staff who showed such thoughtful attentiveness to me for four very challenging days, following the procedure.

I know full well that I am only a drop in the bucket compared to the number of lives all of you have impacted in the course of your careers. And my story could be repeated by countless people across the country and around the world. My story is just one, but, of course, it's the only one I'm qualified to tell.

Finally, I am grateful to the Most High for allowing me something I'm fully persuaded He doesn't owe any of us, and that is continued life. It's His mercy (not His obligation) that I see throughout all of these events. And, for me, I see it as a further extension of the great mercy He showed me many years ago in drawing me into a relationship with Him.

Thanks also to you who took the extraordinary amount of time it must have taken to read all of this. I hope it was useful.

One more recollection from that day that I hadn't included in the original post, is of the unbroken concern I had that began in the ambulance and carried on throughout the entire Cath Lab experience—the concern

I was feeling for Molly. My wife is a tender woman in the best sense of that word. But her tenderness is, without question, matched with stability. To me, these are two of the most beautiful facets of the gem that Molly is. Knowing the strength of her disposition, I wasn't really worried that she would not be able to bounce back if I didn't survive. But somehow I wasn't all that comforted by knowing she would merely *bounce back*.

As I was lying on the Cath Lab table, I found myself overcome with the thought that Molly would even be sad. I love my wife, and I don't *ever* want her to be sad. But of course life doesn't afford such comfort, does it? There I was, completely restrained by my circumstances. I couldn't reach out and touch her face. I couldn't hold her close to me. I couldn't look in her eyes to try to reassure her.

Glancing around the room, the bridge I found, from my restrained state to my tender wife, was a kind soul standing to my left whose eyes of compassion I locked in on over her surgical mask. (I later found out her name was Gretchen.) "Is my wife here?" I asked. "We're working on getting in touch with her." (This confirmed my suspicion that Molly was in fact still at work, unaware.) "What's the password for your phone?" Gretchen asked. I quickly began to tell her, hoping I could finish speaking before losing consciousness again.

Having lost consciousness more than once while in the Cath Lab, I had no clear sense of the passage of time. I just know that at some point, Gretchen looked at me and told me that Molly had arrived. I was so happy, but I was also so worried. With all that was going on, I was afraid that, even being so near, I still might not get to see her again. I tried to articulate through Gretchen what I suspected might very well be my final words to my sweet wife of 26 years: "Tell her that I'm OK. Please. And let her know that even if I'm *not* OK, I'm OK."

I entrusted Gretchen with this message, and she seemed to understand the weight of it, because I saw her eyes well up with tears. I was confident Molly would connect what I was saying with the everlasting comfort I was clinging to—something much deeper and more enduring than my current experience. She would know that my faith is in the Lord and that death would be, in essence, my hopeful passage to my heavenly Home.

Despite the comforting assurance I had in facing death, I was so grateful that I *did* get to see Molly again. I can vividly remember lying there as they wheeled me out, headed for the ICU. Just as we entered the hallway, I glanced up and saw Molly for the first time since this all started. She smiled at me through her tears. You better believe I was smiling too!

11/24/22

HEARTFELT GRATITUDE

2

Following the excitement of November 22nd, I spent the next four days in the hospital. It was during this time that I began feeling a growing desire to get started on an (admittedly) obsessive venture to recognize everyone who saved my life. I wanted to know who the woman was that answered when I dialed 911. Who were the paramedics who resuscitated me in the ambulance? And what were the names of that "flurry" of people working in the Cath Lab?

Since I was still there in the hospital, I figured I'd begin my venture by asking an ICU nurse for the names of the people in the Cath Lab. (I didn't even know if that was allowed, but I had to at least ask.) Fortunately, she provided me with a list of six names: the aforementioned Gretchen, as well as Brittany, Marc, Nicole, Rachel, and last but not least, my new best friend, Dr. Mayuga.

Only two or maybe three people working on me in the Cath Lab that day really stood out in my clouded memory. What *was* clear in my mind, was that each person had an indispensable job and—as you might've guessed by now—I really, really wanted to thank each of them personally. To be honest, I had no intention of giving them a choice in the matter. It's not that I wanted to make anyone feel uncomfortable; I just couldn't imagine containing my gratitude.

As time went by, I assumed I had gotten all of the names of those in the Cath Lab. I was surprised to find out that there was actually one more person. I never figured out why I hadn't gotten their name initially, but the story of how I ended up getting it is worth sharing:

While in the ICU, I received a visit from a long-time friend from Columbus named Andrew. In December, Andrew had been transitioning to a new squadron in the Ohio Air National Guard but had just one final obligation with his previous one. The squadron gathered for dinner at a restaurant near the base. As he walked into the restaurant full of his fellow airmen that night, Andrew noticed there was one seat that remained open at a table, so he sat down. At some point in the course of the evening, he asked one of the men at the table, "Hey, don't you work near Ravenna doing medical work of some kind?" "Yeah, at UH Portage." the man replied. Andrew responded, "I was just up there last Friday visiting a good friend who had a heart attack on Tuesday." And without missing a beat, this man replied, "Oh yeah, the stump grinder!"

So that is how I came to find out that *Josh* was the final missing name of the group of people on duty on November 22nd, in one small section of a relatively small hospital, in a small town in northeast Ohio. And it was discovered at a completely unrelated, final event almost a hundred miles away, weeks later, through an unlikely mutual connection between myself and Josh. And while some might call this nothing more than a coincidence, I can't help but see the hand of providence in it. It was another meaningful reminder that I had not been forgotten even in the small details that, to me, mattered so much.

DECEMBER 1st

After being home from the hospital for about a week, I got behind the wheel for the first time and drove myself to the City of Kent Fire Station to see if I could get the names of the paramedics. I wasn't expecting to be able to speak with anyone in particular, but as it turned out, the person they sent out to the waiting area to talk was none other than one of the men who had performed CPR on me. I was able to get his name, shake his hand, and tell *Tyler* just how much I appreciated what he did for me. As an unexpected bonus, I was able to listen to, and record, his recollection of what happened.

I had assumed that my situation was nothing out of the ordinary for the first responders. I remember even telling Tyler that I didn't know if he'd remember much, knowing they have a lot of calls to deal with. But as I was saying that, Tyler quickly interjected, "Yeah, but your case is interesting because it all happened right in front of us." I listened as he continued to elaborate on what was different about this call—not completely out of the ordinary of course, but there were a few things that were distinctly memorable for him.

As we spoke, I couldn't help but ask about details. Tyler confirmed my recollection about where we were when the first arrest occurred, saying, "Right about 261 and 59 we were like, 'This isn't good.' ... Your EKG went into what's called V-tach. Your heart's going like 200 times a minute, but not efficiently, and then you became cyanotic, so your lips were turning blue and that tells us you're not getting enough oxygen to your brain. And because of the blockages in your heart, you're not getting enough oxygen to the heart muscle. So that's when we have to change gears. That rhythm on the monitor went from V-tach to V-fib. The bottom part of your heart is just going nuts. It's not doing anything productive. So that's when we had to defibrillate you. So we shocked you at 200 joules I think, which is normally where we start."

He continued to fill in the blanks of what happened inside the ambulance: "I did CPR for a couple minutes and then after you came back, you were talking to us. You said, 'I can't see.'" (I assumed this was around the time that everything appeared double-layered.) Tyler continued: "We were super curious about that. You had just gone through a pretty traumatic event so we weren't going to poke and prod, but then you asked us if you were dreaming."

I later learned that the conversation we had in the ambulance was relatively unusual for paramedics. Oftentimes their patients who receive CPR are not able to talk, either because they are unconscious or because they have a breathing tube down their throat—something known as intubation. At other times the patient doesn't *want* to talk because of the intensity of the trauma they are experiencing.

Tyler continued to relay to me what happened after the ambulance arrived at the hospital: "Then we wheeled you in. There were nursing students, there were medics, there were nurses, there were doctors—waiting for us. That's when you went out again, and we shocked you for that second time, but you were awake by the time we got to the room, which was very close. At that point you were able to talk to the doctor. That's when they shipped you to the Cath Lab."

As our conversation continued, more and more of my cloudiness from that day cleared. Up to that point, I had been unsure if I was ever going to be able to have any of the holes in my memory filled in, but Tyler was kind and patient enough to do much of that for me. Suffice it to say, this conversation was an incredibly meaningful part of the healing process.

DECEMBER 12th

I got a call in early December asking if I could receive a visit from a woman named Sara who serves our city as a "Community Para-medicine Provider." What that means, at least in part, is that Sara follows up with people who've been in situations like mine to see if they have any questions regarding medications or other related matters. When Sara came to the house on the 12th, she was accompanied by Chief Myers of the City of Kent Fire Department.

I was so impressed with the fact that such a follow-up program even exists. What an incredible idea to personally check in with residents after they have experienced significant medical trauma. It's such a great way to offer help with *present* needs, while also gathering information that could enable first responders to more effectively and efficiently treat someone *in the future*.

So the first thing that impressed me was the program itself, but I was even more impressed by Sara and Chief Myers. They both asked thoughtful questions and then so patiently listened as I struggled to put into words what all had happened to me. The care and patience they showed was truly exemplary, and I was genuinely grateful for their visit.

DECEMBER 13th

The next day, both Molly and I would have the privilege of meeting the other two men on the call that day—*Paul* and *Greg*. It was great to get to talk with them under, shall we say, *less intense* circumstances. I was so thankful as well that Molly was able to join me this time since she was also processing this whole experience and wanted to convey her gratitude to the men who saved my life.

Greg and Paul told us a couple of sobering things that gave us a lot to think about. The first thing that really caught my attention was when they told us (as did Tyler) that they don't usually see people again who went through what I went through. I wondered about this, and asked if that was because the person doesn't survive, or because they don't stop back in to thank them. "Both."

They went on to share how most of the time a person doesn't survive *one* cardiac arrest, let alone four. But they also shared that those who *do* survive have a lot to adjust to, so oftentimes recovery just sort of takes precedence. *(Six months later, another Kent paramedic named Jordan reiterated this to me vividly as he reached out to shake my hand saying, "I've never met someone who survived 100% blockage of their left anterior descending artery.")*

The second thing that Greg and Paul said that we really had to think about, was the old adage we'd already heard: "We were just doing our jobs." … Hold it. Now, I didn't want to be rude, but let's just say I *strongly* disagreed. There's no way I could reduce what they do to something comparable to me grinding a stump! Oh, I understood the *sentiment*, and I of course knew they weren't suggesting that saving lives isn't important. I could also appreciate the modesty that their sentiment reflected. But the work that they do is so much more significant than what "just a job" would suggest.

One question I received on this visit, that only one or two other people have asked me to this day, was about whether or not I had any recollections from the period of time that my heart was stopped. I loved the question because it's something I would be curious about myself. Everyone has their opinions about NDEs, or "near-death experiences." Mine are pretty loosely held, but from the limited reading I've done, I do think that some of the accounts could be legitimate since some contain factors that would be very hard to explain as simply coincidence or natural occurrence. (Not that I hold to a merely naturalistic worldview anyway.) Unfortunately, my own experience of temporarily dying was probably not technically an NDE. Sorry to disappoint you if you were hoping for something more spectacular.

DECEMBER 20th

One last visit I wanted to make was to the City of Kent Police Station to meet the 911 operator who took my call. While she was reserved with regard to being recognized publicly, I was at least able to give her a gift and briefly express my gratitude for being that vital bridge. As a bonus, I also learned that I could obtain a copy of the actual 911 phone call. I filled out a brief form and received an email with the file. It ended up being healing for me, but also a very surreal thing to listen to.

To wrap things up, I want to acknowledge the remaining collective group of people at the UH Portage Medical Center. I really appreciated the attentive ICU nurses who made those first days and nights in the hospital so much better than they could have been. I'm thankful too for the accomplished Echo Techs who carefully took ultrasound images of my heart so that the doctors could see what damage was done. And lastly, I'm thankful for the caring floor nurses in the step-down unit who kept a watchful eye over me as I recovered sufficiently to return home.

All of these women and men of the City of Kent Fire Department, University Hospitals Portage Medical Center, and the 911 operator made the decision, years before I was privileged to meet them, to enter the noble and sometimes thankless first response and medical fields. They did this so that they could make a difference for people in need. They have. And I want them to know that they are all worthy of my deepest respect.

Representing UH Portage Medical Center

CONTINUING KINDNESS

3

During those long initial days in the hospital, Molly and I experienced what can perhaps best be described as equal parts *relief* and *worry*. We were relieved that my heart was pumping again, that my blood was flowing freely, that my breastbone and ribs weren't broken, and that I never had to be intubated. But I'll admit we were kind of worried about the future.

It seemed like whenever we began to feel the heaviness of that worry though, our spirits would be lifted by kindness from friends and family. Probably a dozen people came to visit us in those first four days. My mom (who had already lost one son) was of course very concerned and spent many hours with us. Other family and friends came to visit us as well. They were *all* a rich blessing to Molly and me. On two occasions, close friends brought their young children along with them. The children were of course fun to see but it was the heartfelt sincerity of Joseph's (and later on Andrew's) prayers for our family that I recall bringing tears to more than just my own eyes.

The inevitable *financial* concerns were of course on my mind, though I hadn't said a word about it to anyone.

(I don't think Molly and I had even discussed it.) I couldn't help but wonder what the emergency services, the hospital care, the rehabilitation process, and the loss of work was going to cost us. I was still confused about what the rehab process would even look like and wondered what follow-up care I would need further down the road. (I also wondered how *far* that road might extend.) I wouldn't say the financial aspect was front-and-center yet, but being self-employed, doing a physically demanding job, I knew the future would probably have some challenges. But before the financial strain could even *become* front-and-center, some other friends stepped in to initiate two individual efforts on our behalf.

Not too long after being released from the hospital, my friend Kris stopped by to visit. He asked if I would be OK with him reaching out to some families we both knew from the church our family had previously been part of. Kris and his wife Lisa were pretty sure that some of those families would like to help us, and he told me that they wanted to do it anonymously.

I was immediately stopped in my tracks by the thoughtfulness and practicality that this offer showed. But then my pride quickly began to creep up and I was reluctant to accept. I didn't want to admit that I *had* any need. In response to that pride, I was confronted in my mind by a loving rebuke I had received from a mentor named Jeff, 30 years ago: "Korey, you need to be willing to receive from people. You shouldn't rob them of the joy of giving." I thought, "OK, Jeff. You're right. I hear you." So I told Kris we would accept anything people would like to do to help us.

Within mere days, Kris reported back how much had already been given, with more on the way. Though I'm really not sure I *had* any expectation, any expectation I *would have had*, was certainly surpassed. The response from these dear families (whom we still have to guess as to their specific identity) meant so much. It's really hard to put into words what it's like to be on the receiving end of such generosity. It's harder still to not be able to personally thank the givers.

Not too long after this, a dear friend named Mike, who also had visited us in the hospital, approached me too. Mike and his wife Heidi had so appreciated what Kris and the generous families from the church had done (as did Molly and I), but knew that using an online fundraising platform would allow others, on a wider circumference, to respond to the need. So Mike asked if we were OK with him setting that up and promoting it. As Jeff's wise rebuke continued to ring in my ears, I again agreed. Mike & Heidi's generosity, in combination with that of many others, was almost more than our hearts could bear. (…in a good way.)

I would be remiss to not mention that a number of other people gave to us wholly apart from these two organized efforts—financially yes, but some came to visit us, some brought delicious meals to lighten our load, and some brought gifts. Molly's employer (and our dear friends) gave her whatever time she needed off work, without hesitation. A friend named Charlie knew what challenges I was having with equilibrium so he just walked with me. (I counted on his past Army medic training in case I had an issue.) All of these extensions of kindness continued to reinforce the message to our hearts that we were abundantly loved.

So it was that, in this season of our worry, when our future was in question in more ways than one, we found ourselves supported through such abundant, continuing kindness. What a gift it was to be reminded of those lessons on worrying that I'd held in my head for a long time: *each day has enough trouble of its own, let tomorrow worry about itself,* and the lesson that, *worrying about the future won't add a single moment to the span of my life.* I actually felt a little disappointed that those lessons had to, once again, bridge that critical distance from my head to my heart, but I was grateful that they had.

GETTING THE WORD OUT

4

Less than a week after coming home from the hospital, I received a call from someone with University Hospitals asking if I was willing to be interviewed about my experience with cardiac arrest. I told them that if what happened to me could make a difference in someone else's life, I would be more than happy to share it. They then asked if I would be open to being interviewed for television if they could line that up. I'll admit I was a little nervous at *that* prospect, but my answer was the same.

After the call, I just continued on with life back home, not knowing if anything would come of the request. But by mid-December, I received a call from Maia Belay of FOX 8 Cleveland. She wanted to know if she and a cameraman could come to the house. So on December 20th I got to meet them both and be interviewed. When it was all done, I thought Maia did a great job of getting to the most beneficial points for viewers to know.

That evening, Molly, Nathan and I gathered in the living room to watch it. While the entire interview process had lasted about an hour, I knew that all of the footage would have to be edited down to just a couple of minutes for television. It came on and, as we sat there, I silently prayed that those two minutes would be multiplied in their impact on viewers.

Reflecting back on something Sara and Chief Myers had brought up, I wondered if the interview might inspire people to learn CPR so they'd be able to save someone's life. If so, that would be incredible! Or perhaps someone else might now think to search for "heart attack symptoms" online just like I did. Whatever fruit the interview would ultimately bear, I felt it was important to get the word out. Of course I have no idea of the full extent of its reach, but I hope that it was beneficial to someone, somewhere.

Please get to know the heart attack warning signs on the next page. If you or someone you observe is having these symptoms, *especially if they come on suddenly and with no apparent explanation*, please call 911.

Common Heart Attack Warning Signs

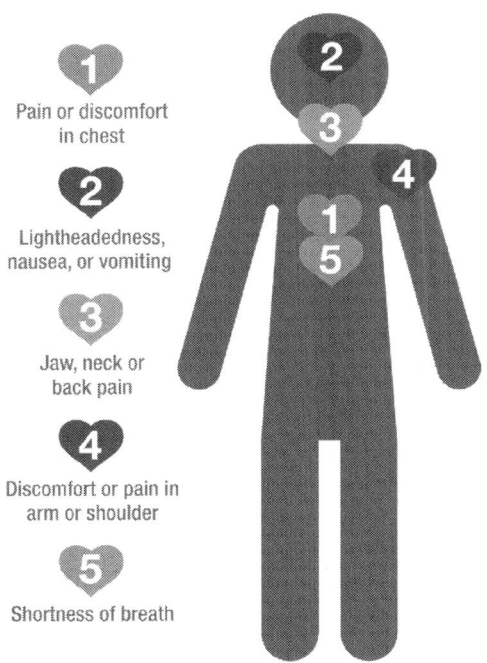

1. Pain or discomfort in chest
2. Lightheadedness, nausea, or vomiting
3. Jaw, neck or back pain
4. Discomfort or pain in arm or shoulder
5. Shortness of breath

Learn more at Heart.org/HeartAttack.

Please be aware that while these warning signs are important, you do not need to have *all five* of them to be in danger. In my case, I only experienced three of them: chest pain (#1), lightheadedness (#2), and shortness of breath (#5), but within 15 minutes, my heart had completely stopped. Additionally, some symptoms *not* included on this diagram may be indicators. For me, sweating profusely—for no apparent reason—was one of the main things that caused me to discount that I was just experiencing indigestion. And finally, blood pressure does not *necessarily* indicate you are, or are not, having a heart attack. That morning my blood pressure was near my normal range at 123 over 82, as shown in this picture that I took about 15 minutes before arresting:

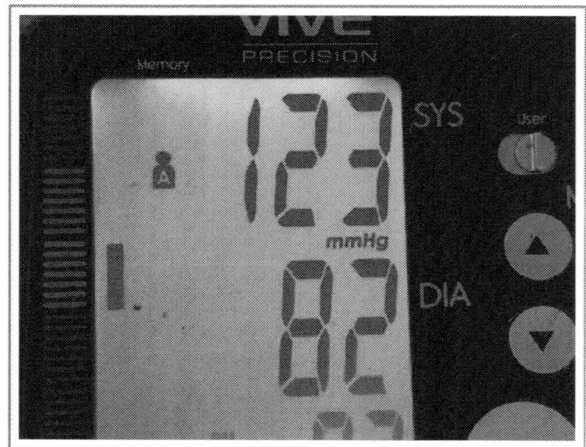

11/22/22 - 11:35 AM

RECOVERY UPDATES

5

The following updates are personal communications which I shared via email as well as on the online fundraising platform. I am including them here unedited. They will provide a continued window into what recovery was like over the first four months.

As you read these, let me reiterate one thing I mentioned in the Introduction. The timeline and events in these updates will not necessarily be the same for *any other* cardiac arrest survivor. There are a number of factors and they can vary significantly from person to person. The first update I wrote was to the group of people that Kris had reached out to, who preferred to remain anonymous. These generous friends supported us without hesitation and I couldn't wait to express to them my appreciation:

12/6/22 Thank You and Update
Dear friends,
We have been both deeply humbled and incredibly uplifted by your kindness to us. We've been brought low with the sense that we aren't deserving, only to be thrust back up with the rich sense that we are loved.

We don't know (yet) who you all are, but we certainly think you need to know that we are so appreciative. When Kris dropped off the compiled amount as a couple of checks, I was quite literally, speechless. As I told Kris later, we expected no such thing. And when he told us he was reaching out to "some Grace families he thought would like to help," we certainly didn't know what that would mean. What it *has* meant is that I will be able to focus so much more on rehabilitating.

I'll share with you an update I just got this morning: I've known for a few days that my cardiologist does in fact want to place a third stent in the artery that caused my cardiac arrests—the left anterior descending artery. The timing of that was up in the air and was causing a bit of anxiety. I found out this morning that the procedure will be done December 21st. The best news being that, following that, I can finally begin rehab. I've been trying to be as active as I can, but am advised by my cardiologist that activity while being monitored by the EKG equipment is the best way to know what I'm able to do at each phase of rehab.

In addition, (and please skip if this is getting too long) one of the other big concerns is my lack of any minutes of deep sleep whatsoever. I've had moderate to severe, obstructive sleep apnea for who knows how long, and had an Inspire Therapy device implanted in my chest in 2016 to address it. It stimulates the nerve in my tongue while I sleep to negate the obstruction so I can breathe normally and achieve the restorative "deep sleep" that is so important. (You can look into the impact of a chronic lack of deep sleep if you're interested.) My concern has been that the four defibrillations I received short-circuited the device, so I haven't dared try to activate it at night. The update here is that Molly and I will be going to the Cleveland Clinic on Tuesday, Dec. 13th to hopefully get some direction.

Finally, if (as I'm assuming) you all know Molly and/or me, you know that I would want to hug each and every one of you to connect and to thank you. We are both incredibly grateful and deeply moved by the way you have shown us such loving-kindness at this interesting time in our lives.

Correction: the additional stent was actually needed in the right coronary artery (RCA), not in the left anterior descending artery (LAD).

As Mike & Heidi's online fundraising campaign was gaining steam, we were yet again deeply moved by people's generosity. Some people gave allowing us to know who they were, while many gave anonymously here too. I wanted to provide this *new* group of people with an update on how we were doing.

Amidst the encouragement that this support was though, I found myself beginning to have some mild anxiety about a second, upcoming catheterization procedure. We were also eagerly anticipating our daughter's return from Naval training. She was due to arrive home barely ten hours before my catheterization was scheduled to begin.

1/11/23 Thank You and Update
Since I don't know who many of the generous people are who have supported us recently, I wanted to express my gratitude and also provide an update. This is that update…

As I considered again today the remarkable generosity of each one of you, I was again overcome with a wave of emotions. Granted, some of the emotional sensitivity I'm experiencing these days is part of the aftermath of what happened. But so much of what I'm feeling as I write this even now is just immense gratitude for so many people who would actually give to our family so selflessly.

We know things are tight for everyone, and we don't take for granted what it took for each of you to help us to be able to take a breath (make that a few breaths) as I anxiously await cardiac rehab beginning on January 17th, assuming no more setbacks. In addition to my gratitude, I also wanted to offer an update to anyone who might want that: (I'll briefly start from the top.)

11/22/22 - the cardiac arrests that began this whole "saga", as my LAD (left anterior descending) artery became 100% blocked, leading to four episodes of cardiac arrest, and the life-saving measures exercised by the City of Kent Fire Department and the UH Portage Cath Lab. No need for any more detail on this!

12/21/22 - a scheduled catheterization that went from a routine, 30-45 min, single stent procedure for my RCA (right coronary artery) which turned into a three-hour emergency situation due to an unexpected dissection (tearing of the inner artery wall) resulting in three additional stents. To my surprise, the mental impact of this experience, in some ways, was greater than (or perhaps layered on top of) the Nov. 22 cardiac arrests.

Because I had to be kept awake throughout this procedure, I was fully aware when something began to go wrong, but no one could tell me what it was. ... no fault to them. I was crippled with fear as I lay on the Cath Lab table. I just had to watch and listen as more people came in to help fix the problem.

My cardiologist, Dr. Mayuga, (who also did my stents in November) did an absolutely remarkable job on this day too. Once things settled down, she actually told me she was praying for me, which was a statement that moved me to tears with gratitude while simultaneously sinking my heart. It did so because it conveyed just how close I came again to a very desperate situation. She later confided that they were very close to flying me up to UH main campus for open heart surgery.

12/30/22 - the Friday before New Year's when I began feeling chest pain that was very reminiscent (though less intense) of Nov. 22nd. I found myself in a similar state of denial to that day in November. I couldn't handle not being able to discern what I should do. I only came to accept that something bad was happening because our neighbor and friend Clete (who manages cardiac rehab at Summa in Akron) came over to check on me, ultimately advising me to take a nitro pill. The pain and anxiety subsided some until later that evening when I called 911 instead of calling him again—as he had advised me to do if the pain returned. I got to see one of the original trio who saved my life this time too, as they transported me back to UH Portage.

Shortly after arriving, I was informed that the elevated troponin levels (a protein released into the bloodstream when the heart is under distress) would keep me from being released until a third catheterization could be done to see what was going on. (Due to the holidays, they were aiming for Tuesday, Jan. 3rd.) I stayed in the hospital connected to yet another blood thinner in order to keep heart attacks at bay. Finally, on Tuesday evening, I ended up being transported to UH main campus in Cleveland to have the catheterization done. That way, if open heart surgery was needed, I would already be where it could be done.

As Wednesday came, the anxiety over going back into a Cath Lab was almost unbearable. I called a dear friend in Chicago that morning, unable to speak, as I wept over the phone in the darkness of the early morning. He consoled me in love, reassured me in faith, and advised me in the truth.

Thanks to a few things: the prayers of caring friends, a playlist of calming songs, and what seemed to be a more generous level of sedative this time, the catheterization came and went in a relatively uneventful way! Hallelujah! I was so grateful the outcome was, by comparison, a breeze. As it turns out, I was having a 90% blockage in a side artery, and they concluded that it would not be treated with another stent, but with an additional medication. (… taking me up to seven).

This brings me to my final piece in all this that I want to share: if you are a praying person, please pray for my body to adjust to these medications. They leave me, at times, straining to breathe and often fighting dizziness if I stand for too long or stand up too quickly. Please pray as well for my mind to heal. I intend to connect with some qualified counsel soon, to help me further process all of this. If you'll permit me, may I share two examples of how this has taken its toll on my mind, so you might better understand the impact these situations can have on a person?

The first example is what I'm calling "survivor's guilt". (I think this is a term, though I really don't know.) All I can tell you is, it snuck up on me one day while listening to the paramedics. What I mean by "survivor's guilt" is, as I began to hear so many paramedics comment on how unusual it was for me to have survived, I was overwhelmed by the reality of what that meant for so many other families: their loved ones *did not* survive. Knowing that, just crushed me. …it still crushes me. Why did I get to survive when so many don't?

These less personal accounts from paramedics were then followed up by a story from our son, that was closer to home. He told me of a co-worker whose father (the exact same age as me) died of just a single episode of cardiac arrest a mere week after mine. You would perhaps think these stories would bring a feeling of relief in the sense that, "You sure have lots to be thankful for, by comparison!" I assure you, hearing these stories does not bring any such sense of relief. It just breaks my heart.

The second (and last) example I will share of how my mind needs to heal, is related to my sleep. The experience of losing consciousness felt (in my case) like falling into, and then being brought back out of, sleep. So you can probably guess what falling asleep feels like now as compared to before.

The first night in ICU, I slept in increments of seconds. Each time, falling asleep only to be jolted awake by the memory of temporarily dying in the ambulance and at the hospital. Thankfully, the battle is less intense now and I can at least get some adequate sleep, but recovery feels so slow when my body won't yield to much-needed rest because my mind is telling it to stay alert.

(I really don't mean to sound like I'm complaining about my situation. Truly. I only want to help anyone who, hopefully, will never experience this, to better understand it.)

I'll let those two examples suffice, but I'm sure you can appreciate what needs to happen moving forward. I'm leaning on the Lord. I'm leaning on friends and family. And I'm leaning on the support you each have given, which will unquestionably make our journey forward more bearable. Thank you. I mean that. To each one of you, thank you from the bottom of my heart.

The friend I called in Chicago was Jeff, the mentor I had mentioned in chapter three. In addition to his listening ear and guidance that early morning, I also reached out to musician and author, Michael Card by email. Though in the middle of leading a tour in Israel, Michael replied that the tour group would pray for me that day. I highly respect both of these men. Their availability and support provided a clear measure of peace in those dark moments as I was mentally preparing for that third visit to the Cath Lab.

The song playlist I mentioned in this update included:
- *Freedom* - Michael Card
- *He's All You Need* - Steve Camp
- *Give Me Jesus* - as sung by Fernando Ortega
- *There's A Stirring* - Caedmon's Call
- *Hello My Old Heart* - The Oh Hello's
- *I Know That My Redeemer Lives* - as sung by Bob Bennett

. . . .

On January 17th, I finally had my first Cardiac Rehab appointment. It felt like the greatest thing since sliced bread! That nagging internal question: *What can I do safely?,* was finally beginning to get answered.

On the mental side of things, I had been really struggling with some crippling doubt about my own discernment. I couldn't seem to stop thinking about how close I had come to *not* calling 911 that day. (If I had waited another ten minutes or so to call, I'd be dead.) It took a close friend and mentor named Bruce to remind me that, while yes I *could* have called sooner, I did *ultimately* make the right decision. And on top of that, I had made other sound decisions about seeking help in the days since the arrests. This reminder was a comforting reassurance I really needed to accept so that I wouldn't collapse under the weight of my own feelings of personal inadequacy.

About Cardiac Rehab (and a surprise bonus), I would later write:

> **1/23/23 Update**
>
> It's weird to come to the realization that some things in life are equal parts discouraging and encouraging. It's discouraging to see just how far from functioning "normally" you really are—getting lightheaded and out of breath from doing minimal work. It's hard to see your muscle mass visibly decrease from just two months of relative inactivity. It's discouraging to not know when you can resume providing for your family. And of course no one wants to be told during winter in Ohio, "No, you're still not cleared to be shoveling snow."
>
> For two months, it has felt like time was riding on the back of a two-legged turtle. It's a challenge to wait patiently to begin a process that will finally transform your "best guess" as to what your heart is actually doing, into the visible beats of your heart on a screen while engaged in activity. It can be agonizing to guess if that sensation in your chest—that seems so unsettling—is just because your blood pressure is low

or because your heart is about to stop again. Overreaction or legitimate concern?

But forget all of that discouraging news, because this past Tuesday, I was finally able to begin the cardiac rehab process at UH Portage and I couldn't be happier about it! That two-legged turtle finally crossed the finish line! I have a caring cardiac rehab specialist who discussed my rehab goals and took me for a timed, EKG-connected walk to establish a baseline.

At the end of that appointment, I mentioned that, in addition to the physical rehabilitation, I really needed some skilled psychological guidance to help with healing the effects this has all had on my mind. I wondered if there was any way I could meet with someone who also understood the particular effects of cardiac trauma on the mind. Those odds seemed slim, but it couldn't hurt to ask could it?

This morning marked my third of 36 rehab appointments, and following this morning's appointment, I had an hour-and-a-half long meeting with a man named Joel whose background is "cardiovascular psychophysiology". You read that right. This man actually specializes in the way physical trauma to the heart affects the mind! As amazing as that is, I do have a personal problem receiving advice (of the sort that will alter the course of my life) from someone who has a fundamentally different worldview than my own.

Well, as I sit here writing this 12 hours later, I'm still floored by how absolutely perfect the meeting was. In fact, after I shared some details of the meeting with Molly, her exact words were, "That's not just an answer to prayer; it's a huge, abundant answer to prayer!" I couldn't agree more. Not only was this man's professional training and psychological background exactly what I needed, but his theological worldview was as close of a match to my own as divinely possible.

There's a lot left to work through, but I see my body recovering strength and endurance. And it was also good to finally be reassured that I'm not, in fact, crazy. …I'll take it.

The predictable rotation through the four machines at rehab felt so reassuring! The recumbent stair-stepper, the stationary bike, the arm pedal machine, and the treadmill, became the mini "mountains" I would scale three times a week. Each one allowed me to regain my confidence, stamina, strength, and balance in their own way.

My balance in particular was a critical factor. You see, equilibrium issues—brought on by the medications—had made walking on normal, solid ground a challenge. So you can probably guess then what walking on *moving ground* (treadmill) felt like. But I would discover that this too was therapy. My body needed to face strange sensations and challenges to my equilibrium in order to reorient itself under its new conditions.

As I made progress physically, I finally had a budding glimmer of hope. It enabled me to feel more and more confident that my mind might actually heal too. And there were also signs that our family's future might be coming into some measure of focus. A month later, I wrote:

2/22/23 Update

I was asked if I could offer another update for those who have cared for and supported us, which I was more than happy to do. As I sat down to write, I noticed that today is exactly 3 months from a day that, for the rest of the world likely has very little significance, but for me personally, I'll never forget. So much has happened in those 3 months. There have been many moments I can only describe as deeply unsettling. But there have been an equal number of moments where I've truly sat in awe at the lavish grace we've been shown.

I won't rehash, or even refer back to, the whole chain of initial and subsequent events. I'll just say that, for me, this season of my life has revealed just how much I benefit from truly understanding what's going on around and within me. As an example, one of the biggest things I longed for, following my cardiac arrests, was to be hooked up to an EKG while doing various activities. Well, this morning I completed 16 of 36 sessions of cardiac rehab, and I am still overjoyed to be able to go.

Every Monday, Wednesday, and Friday at UH Portage, I work out on four machines for an increasing amount of time and intensity each. They have a very encouraging and capable staff there as well as a fun group of patients. (And who doesn't want to be the "youngster" in the room?) The entire time I'm working out, a remote EKG is monitored by a nurse and thankfully it is now consistently showing "sinus rhythm". (In the cardiac sense, "sinus" comes from the sinoatrial node, which is a region of cardiac muscle.) I'm really happy to see the progress thus far and I find myself feeling hopeful for the future.

But hope, more often than not, lives alongside uncertainty. And I would say a couple of issues have my attention the most. The first is the uncertainty of the next phase of life for us. There are quite a few facets to this, but one nagging one is the continuing adjustment to meds that so generously treat me to their side effects. Don't get me wrong—I am super grateful for the medications! They allow my blood to continue to do its thing rather than stage a "sit-in" at the site of my stents. But having to check my balance due to lightheadedness, *every single time* I stand up, does get tiring some days.

The second issue is my sleep. Having obstructive sleep apnea, in the moderate-to-severe category takes its toll on—among other things—the heart. In 2016, I was equipped with an implant that kept my airway unobstructed while I slept. That is until I was shocked back to life several times in November. (Again, not complaining!) Inspire Therapy (the implant of which I speak) is tough, but it wasn't *that* tough. And due to my medical situation, I can't have any surgeries for a year. ...so no replacement until the end of 2023 at the earliest. I'll keep trying to fight for quality sleep with whatever methods I can find, but as anyone else with a sleep disorder can tell you, it's a bit of a challenge.

Well, that's probably enough for you to have to read. So, again, let me sincerely express my continuing gratitude to all those who have supported us in so many heartfelt ways. And I honestly look forward to serving others from the abundance of kindness we've felt so meaningfully these past three months.

In case you're wondering, coronary stents are small mesh tubes that hold arteries open. They may be constructed of various materials, and in time (generally 6-12 months) tissue grows over the stent as the body accepts them. During this time, medications are taken to reduce the chances of blood clotting at the site of the stents. While these medications may bring on some of the side effects I mentioned in the updates above, they are vital to take throughout the entire process.

* *

One final update:

3/7/23 Update
I am told these updates are helpful for those who would like to read them, and for those who have too

much going on to be able to, they can very easily skip them.

I wanted to share four developments that have been significant:

1) Last Friday, I completed cardiac rehab in half the time expected. While the UH Portage rehab staff was remarkable to work with, an unforeseen, difficult circumstance led to wrestling with the question of whether or not I would be better off continuing rehabilitating from home, self-supervised. The decision to rehab from home made sense due to the amount of progress I'd made in regaining strength and losing weight. (It also helped that I hadn't had any further cardiac incidents.) I've still got a ways to go, but I'm hopeful as I continue.

2) Just yesterday I completed all necessary documents to begin counseling to help me work through the mental experience of dying and being revived, some of the impact of which (I'm told by a professional), is exacerbated by a life-long struggle with anxiety and depression. I'm seeing how really true it is that we inevitably bring the whole of who we are—struggles as well as strengths—to each new season that we face.

3) Last Wednesday I officially sold the stump grinding business I began a few years ago. This is a

blessing, knowing that the physical strain of that particular type of work may not be best for my (at least immediate) future. This is also a bit scary, not knowing what my own income for my family will be. I have leads and opportunities, but I have to be somewhat cautious in how, and when, I proceed because of adjustments I'm still making with regard to medications and recovery.

4) Finally, I received some affirming news about one of the career tracks I believe could be a wonderful fit. It would take us to another county, but not another state like one of the other options I've been considering would. I am hoping that, by the end of this week, or next week, I'll be able to apply. I was told by the man who oversees the department I'd be in, that they hope to hire "soon".

For my praying friends, I covet your intercession, particularly about our next steps as a family. For non-praying friends, I value your concern as well and am grateful for all of you who have stood in our corner over the past three and a half months.

In His grace,
Korey

RECOVERY ADJUSTMENTS

6

It always seemed to surprise me, as I continued through the recovery phase, just how often I had to make adjustments. As I thought this through, a couple of things occurred to me. The first was that adjusting is just part of life, for *all* of us. Secondly, I realized that my adjustments did not deserve to even be compared to the hardships that many people face. For some, being able to make an adjustment would be a welcomed change, because they are locked into a much harder and more permanent challenge where adjusting isn't even an option. But, with that said, cardiac arrest survival does have its share of adjustments, and since *comparing* them isn't particularly helpful, I'll just *share* them:

CONFINEMENT
There were several, but my first *confinement* (as I'll impolitely call it), was a room within the Intensive Care Unit of the hospital. Within my room, confinement also took the form of a standard hospital bed. Getting out of bed on my own was not permitted, and the side rails kept me from falling out accidentally. Multiple IVs, which provided a steady supply of everything from saline to

medications, would have made it a challenge to get very far anyway.

Not having had much experience with hospital beds, I got to discover that those beds really aren't designed with comfort as their *top* priority. They do offer valuable features such as being able to raise and lower your legs and torso independently. But they're also designed with the priorities of medical treatment and durability over and against what you may be used to at home such as a *comfortable mattress,* pillows that *support*, and sheets that *stay in place.*

By my second day in the ICU, I began to have pretty serious back pain and even muscle spasms. The physical trauma of being on the receiving end of CPR and defibrillation was no doubt more to blame than the hospital bed. Nonetheless, confinement can be a challenging thing to deal with.

FOOD AND WEIGHT LOSS

After confinement, the next adjustment that I recall noticing was a dramatic change in my appetite, resulting in weight loss. In the first couple of weeks, food looked pretty surreal just like everything else. I also looked at food with suspicion, knowing it probably played a role in my cardiovascular condition, so I basically had little interest in it. Within a few weeks, this phenomenon was fading, and, by that time, the doctor's orders to eat a heart-healthy diet had become my guide. I was losing weight pretty quickly.

You'd think that for someone like me who has battled the merciless scale his whole life, losing a lot of weight would be great, but, much to my surprise, losing it so rapidly was a disconcerting challenge. Dropping about 40 pounds in four months made me pause as I looked at myself in the mirror sometimes. (Remember that this wasn't too far from the period of time when *everything* I looked at seemed strange.) Also, since food can be such a big part of our day-to-day lives, a major diet change can be kind of like grieving the loss of an old friend. Even though I knew I was making a *new* friend, we weren't very close yet.

The final thing I'll say about the weight loss adjustment was particular to our family's situation, but it may be relatable. As I lost so much weight, I found myself often thinking back over the previous year as, with steady grief, we watched my beloved mother-in-law decline with cancer before ultimately succumbing to it. I suppose the experience of constantly pushing her to eat, as her weight dropped so rapidly, must've subconsciously altered how I perceived losing weight. I had never before realized how weight loss can, at times, be a sign of decline rather than improvement.

Oddly enough, I even found myself wondering, "Wait. Do I have cancer too?" It surprised me that I would have to ground my concern about this, since nothing objective pointed to me having cancer. And please know I didn't bring anyone else into my passing concern. It was entirely a private matter. I hadn't even told anyone about it until just now. But it *was* another adjustment I didn't expect to have to make.

SCHEDULES

You should know that these sorts of medical emergencies, like most things in life, don't have the common decency to wait for our schedules to clear. For us, my arrests occurred while our 19-year-old daughter was in Navy "A School," which is the Navy's first level of schooling following Basic Training. The reality of being 1,200 miles away, when her dad almost died, was very upsetting for her and for us. We cried together when I first told her over FaceTime what had happened. (I used FaceTime to call because I felt she needed to have the reassurance of seeing my face *before* being told what had happened.) Incidentally, four months after the arrests, our son flew the same 1,200 miles away for Air Force Basic Training. Fortunately, by this time it was much easier.

In addition, both my wife *and* my mom lost their mothers less than six months before my arrests. Those losses, compounded with this new burden that I felt I was putting on them, seemed like an excessive and unfair weight for them to have to bear. But life is like that. It doesn't wait for our permission to be given burdens to carry. Interestingly, Molly recently shared with me that she felt like it was actually a mercy that her mom's death and my arrests didn't coincide. Her comment reminded me that so much of how we experience trials really is a matter of perspective.

NEW MEDICATIONS

I've already shared in the updates about some of the side effects I encountered from taking new meds. But there is also a burden that comes with adjusting to any new routine. Adding one that requires essentially perfect adherence just multiplies that burden. The importance of not missing a single pill for an entire year, was emphasized so much in the hospital that I knew preparing for this new routine was something I had to take seriously.

To help you understand how it went, I'll just open a little window on the way my anxious mind thought all of this through. And to really help you relate, imagine that all of a sudden *you* have to begin taking five or six "can't miss" medications in addition to whatever meds you already take. You'll have to take four in the morning, two in the evening, and one more just before bedtime because taking it then is more effective.

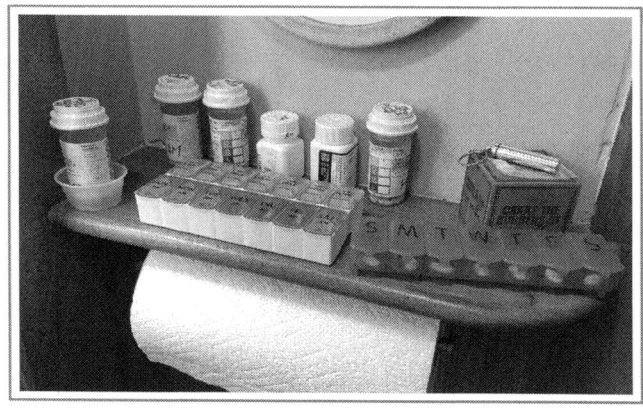

For me, the thought process felt like a barrage of questions coming at me:

- *Should I keep the pills in their original bottles or store them in a weekly pill planner so I can better tell that I've taken them each day?*
- *Should I add the one chewable tablet to the pill planner or should I keep it separate?*
- *But what if keeping the chewable tablet separate jeopardizes remembering to take it?*
- *How will I remember to take my pills at the right time each day?*
- *Should I set three alarms each day to remind me?*
- *If I'm not sure whether or not I took a pill, because I suspect it might've dropped on the floor, should I risk missing a dose or risk taking it twice?*

When that last one actually happened, I called the fire station on their non-emergency line and asked what they would recommend. I was advised that it was probably safer to risk *not* taking it one time rather than taking it twice. Pro-tip: putting each dose of pills in a small cup, and taking them from the cup (like they do in the hospital) will reduce the chance of any pills falling and thus disappearing for all eternity.

I don't want to give the wrong impression here. I'm not at all suggesting that this "barrage of questions" was somehow insurmountable. In a sense, they were just another set of questions that needed to be answered in order to keep moving forward.

MENTAL HEALTH

The challenge of adjusting to the logistics of taking so many new meds is certainly a factor. But what I found to be surprisingly more significant was the *mental* burden associated with taking them. To elaborate, I'll share (with Molly's permission) just one experience we had with this:

A few weeks after being home, while my emotions were still incredibly raw, I asked Molly if she'd be willing to help me by putting two week's worth of my medications into my weekly pill planners because I was so tired and didn't want to mess it up. Being someone who is typically less detail-oriented than I am, I emphasized several times how important it was that she put each pill in each compartment for each day. Of course Molly was glad to help.

A few days later, it was time to begin taking the next week's round of medications. I looked in that first day's compartment only to find that not one, but multiple meds were missing! I opened the second day and the third… the same thing! Well, (and I say this to my shame) I fell apart. I actually started questioning her as if she had done something sinister to sabotage my recovery! In the back of my mind, I *knew* nothing could be further from the truth. But, in that moment, with the weight of the responsibility to perfectly take my meds weighing on my already depleted mind, I actually doubted the love and loyalty of my sweet wife. And we're talking about a woman who had shown me nothing but generous loving-kindness for 26 years! Although she was gracious and forgave me, I was crushed by my lack of charity towards her. I wept because I was so troubled by how poorly I was handling this life that I had been given back.

You might recall from the updates, that I got to meet with a guy whose area of specialty is *cardiovascular psychophysiology*. Before all of this happened, I had no idea such a specialty even existed. Now I understand why it does. Healing through prior mental battles, such as anxiety or depression, can be challenging, while some mental battles may be entirely new, brought on simply by the health crisis itself. But just like the mental factors that we bring to a major health event, we also bring our own set of pre-existing *physical* complications.

PHYSICAL HEALTH

Going through this experience, I came to realize that very few people encounter major medical events with a clean slate. Most of us no doubt have prior health factors, both mental *and* physical, that will play a role. These were the physical ones for me:

- Sleep apnea. Since I covered this in the updates, I won't say any more about it here.

- GERD: The main symptom of Gastroesophageal Reflux Disease is heartburn, which is a painful burning sensation in the middle of your chest. Also, for many people, heartburn can get worse when they recline, which can make it hard to get a good night's sleep.

- Headaches: After about 35 years of battling headaches almost daily, I was thrilled that, for whatever reason, headaches were no longer a chronic problem for about a year prior to my arrests. This was great until I found out that one of my new medications brought them roaring back.

- <u>Fibromyalgia</u>: An autoimmune disorder characterized by widespread musculoskeletal pain as well as fatigue, fibromyalgia can be accompanied by sleep, memory, and mood issues as well. Normal pain sensations are amplified, apparently due to the way the brain and spinal cord process signals related to pain.

- <u>Tooth Infection</u>: This one might seem unrelated at first, but during my time in the Intensive Care Unit, I began experiencing pain in my gums near one tooth in particular. One nurse cautioned me that an infection in my bloodstream could become serious and advised that I talk to the doctor about getting on an antibiotic. In addition to the concern about infection, not being able to have any form of surgery (such as tooth extraction) for a year because of blood thinners, has made that one tooth an ongoing issue for now.

I'm certainly not suggesting that any of these factors are particularly exceptional health issues. Many people have *much more* difficult ones. I only want to highlight the fact that, when we come to any major medical crisis, we bring with us all that we are dealing with, and sometimes those things can exacerbate the primary issue.

EQUILIBRIUM

I never expected my balance to be such a lingering issue. Even months after arresting, just going for a simple walk wasn't exactly simple. Molly and I have always liked to walk each evening on a trail near our house, but I soon discovered there's a spot along the trail (where it intersects a road) that the grade changes so abruptly I had trouble even looking at it. The worst equilibrium problems though still occur when I stand up too quickly, particularly from squatting down. As I understand it, this is a condition known as orthostatic hypotension, where your blood pressure drops when standing up.

NEW SENSATIONS
In the midst of these other adjustments, I discovered a new game—one that's honestly gotten pretty *old* now at six months. I like to call it, *Guess That Sensation!* (Can you hear the game show music?) As you might've suspected, the most concerning sensations are almost always associated with my chest, which has had some degree of sensitivity constantly since the arrests. As the soreness fluctuates in intensity, trying to discern if I'm feeling *pain* (more serious) or *pressure* (less serious) has been anybody's guess.

Because of having to be relatively idle for so long after the arrests, when I would work my arms, it usually resulted in some shoulder discomfort—#4 on the "warning signs" diagram. I could usually assume, without much concern, that the shoulder discomfort was nothing to worry about. But it was something I always had to pause to assess.

I'm not much of a coffee or tea drinker, so I rarely drink anything particularly hot. But I found that when I *did* swallow hot drinks or soup, it felt a lot like chest pain as it ran down my esophagus. Drinks that were extra cold sometimes set off the same sensation.

And finally, there was the sensation of straining to breathe that I mentioned in the updates. I had to really stop and try to guess what was going on when that one would happen. Since not being able to breathe is associated with dying (obviously), it aroused a lot of fear until I came to realize it would stop in about ten seconds, so I needn't worry. The fact that it would repeat—sometimes within a few minutes and other times with hours between—meant I got to practice *not worrying* quite a bit! Fortunately this sensation eased significantly after I was taken off one of my meds due to having lost so much weight.

As time went on, the guesswork on *all* of these sensations became rooted in knowledgeable experience. I learned that the sensations would come and go with greater distance between, but I'm not sure there is any real shortcut on the journey with these types of sensations. It just seems to be an unavoidable part of the recovery process.

FIRSTS

One of the common elements of any life-altering event, whether it's the death of a loved one or a major medical incident, is the impact of so many significant *firsts* that follow. When someone loses a spouse for instance, the first anniversary, birthday, or significant holiday following their death is usually really tough. This phenomenon, following a health scare, can be very similar.

In my case, the *first*, first I recall was when we arrived home after I was released from the hospital. As we pulled into the driveway, I sat there in the passenger seat, frozen for about a minute. I looked over at the front door and recalled the last time I had walked through it. Once inside, walking across the dining room floor where I had laid down half-expecting to die felt strange too. And most recently, when I grabbed my work boots for the first time, I literally stopped and just stared at them. It was almost as if I was looking at them for the first time. I had completely forgotten that my laces had been cut to shreds in the Cath Lab as part of saving my life.

Throughout these firsts, (and a whole lot more like them) I found it helpful to think of them in perspective. I'm no mathematician, but I'm pretty sure we only have to do the firsts, *one* time. Each *first* is followed by a *second*, which is followed by a *third*, and so on.

HABITS

One final adjustment I discovered was that new habits had to form while old ones needed to be set aside. One strange new habit I had to quickly adjust to was carrying a supply of nitroglycerin pills with me wherever I went, in case I needed to quickly increase blood flow. Another one was having to keep my toes and fingers warmer since they were now much colder than ever before. Sometimes it still takes most of the night—even under extra blankets—for my toes to not feel ice cold. I'm pretty sure this is another side effect of the meds. Of course old habits—such as having a big bowl of whatever kind of ice cream I wanted, whenever I felt like it, or salting my food without reservation—are hard habits to say goodbye to.

But perhaps the most surprising habit adjustment for me occurred the day I instinctively reached out to lock our front door. You see, before the arrests, when I was home alone, I would often lock the front door when laying down for a nap. But as I stood there, it occurred to me that if I lock the door and have to call 911 again, the paramedics will be delayed getting inside the house. Thus, I had to exchange one concern—that of someone getting inside the house, with the opposite concern—that of someone *not being able to* get inside the house. It felt so strange to be forced to take notice of some of these otherwise unnoticed habits.

If this chapter felt a bit heavier than previous ones, allow me to apologize. Some of the heaviness is unavoidable since certain adjustments were difficult and I don't want to pretend that they weren't. My primary hope in sharing these adjustments is that anyone who might go through a similar situation would recognize them as a very normal thing to be expected.

CAUSE(S)

7

So, what exactly caused my heart to arrest? Well, the *immediate* cause was that I had a heart attack due to plaque erupting and stopping the blood flow in my left anterior descending ("widow maker") artery, and this caused my heart to arrest. But perhaps you're wondering, as I still am—what caused the plaque to build up and my arteries to narrow in the first place? As you already know, I'm no expert, but the more I've read up on cardiac issues, the more convinced I am that *multiple* factors were actually involved, and the hard truth is, I'll probably never know for sure which ones were *more* to blame than others.

Shifting from me to people in general, there are a couple of contributing factors to cardiovascular health that we cannot control, but there are many other ones that we *can* control. If it helps to think of them divided that way, please consider the following lists. As you do, please consider what changes you might need to make:

FACTORS *OUTSIDE* OF OUR CONTROL:
* **Genetics** - Hereditary factors can range from gene mutations to a predisposition to high blood pressure.

- **Childhood Trauma** - *Adverse Childhood Experiences* (ACEs) have been linked to compromised cardiac health as well as other serious health issues. Many of us have experienced ACEs ourselves. Helping children through, *or out of*, these situations is incredibly important, but the sad reality is that help does not always arrive until after some amount of damage has been done.

FACTORS *WITHIN* OUR CONTROL:

- **Stress** - Stressful situations in life aren't always controllable, but managing their effects often is, at least to some degree.
- **Chronic Sleep Deprivation** - A lack of deep sleep can lead to high blood pressure (hypertension), anxiety, depression, stroke, obesity, etc.
- **Poor Diet** - A diet too high in sodium, highly processed carbohydrates, and both saturated and trans fats can lead to coronary heart disease.
- **Obesity** - Excessive body fat can lead to high blood pressure and can cause fatty material to build up in the arteries.
- **Disease** - While we may *attempt* to avoid all disease, our efforts are no guarantee, and certain diseases will impact cardiovascular health. Covid-19 is just one recent example.

- **Diabetes** - High blood sugar from diabetes can damage blood vessels and the nerves controlling the heart. Diabetics are more likely to have other conditions that elevate the risk for heart disease as well.

- **High Blood Pressure** - Hypertension can damage your arteries by making them less elastic, decreasing the flow of blood and oxygen to your heart.

- **Tobacco Use** - Nicotine constricts blood vessels and can cause an increase in blood pressure, accelerate your heart rate, and increase the flow of blood to the heart. It can also harden your arteries.

- **Blood Cholesterol Levels** - While good cholesterol (High-Density Lipoprotein or, HDL) is beneficial, Low-Density Lipoprotein (LDL) can develop fatty deposits in the blood vessels.

- **Physical Inactivity** - Being physically inactive decreases heart muscle strength and leads to other contributing factors like obesity, high blood pressure, and diabetes.

- **Excessive Alcohol Consumption** - Drinking too much alcohol can increase both heart rate and blood pressure, and can lead to weakened heart muscle and an irregular heartbeat.

- **Poor Oral Health** - Studies seem to suggest that excess tooth plaque may indicate excessive plaque in the circulatory system as well. Also, bacteria brought on by gum disease may enter the bloodstream and infect vulnerable heart valves.

As you can see, there are a lot of factors to address. At times we may not address them because of a lack of knowledge. However, I'll confess that sometimes the problem is less a matter of ignorance and more about being *unwilling* to act. For the factors within our control, we have an obligation to take action! Do it because your life matters—for you and also for those who need you.

ONE VERY RARE CAUSE:

Commotio cordis - This phenomenon takes place when a sudden, blunt impact to the chest occurs at a particularly critical point during a heartbeat cycle, regardless of a person's cardiovascular health. (The reason it's so rare is that the impact must occur within a narrow window of about 40 milliseconds within the cardiac electrical cycle.) Though extremely uncommon, it's very serious, causing sudden death if not treated within just a few minutes.

On January 2nd, 2023, NFL player Damar Hamlin experienced commotio cordis on the football field during a nationally televised game. Damar's event occurred exactly 41 days after my own arrests. In fact, I was in the hospital awaiting my third catheterization as I watched, able to relate on some level with Damar's experience. Along with millions of other people, I too prayed for Damar and his family as he was given CPR and his heartbeat restored. Because his cardiac arrest was not due to cardiovascular disease, my timeline for recovery will be different than his I suspect.

The factors I've listed here are important to consider, but they are hardly the final word on the matter. Medical science (like all science) is provisional, which means it should always be acquiring a more accurate and complete understanding of the truth. Because of that, our most complete knowledge of the contributing factors of heart disease should be available at the time you are *reading* this, not at the time that I am *writing* it. For the most current understanding of all of the various causes, you could start your research with these reliable resources:

* The American Heart Association: heart.org
* American College of Cardiology: cardiosmart.org
* British Heart Foundation: bhf.org.uk

My ultimate hope with this brief chapter on the causes of cardiac arrest, is that it will motivate you to respond. For even if we were able to know everything there is to know about the causal factors, that would still not be enough. To make any sort of difference, we have to *do something productive* with that knowledge. Don't worry about perfection; just continue to aim for *progress*. Believe me—if I can make progress, so can you!

After this upcoming, final chapter, I've included some space for you to write down a few things that you may want to do to address your own heart health.

HEREAFTER

8

You might be wondering what lies beyond the first six months of recovery. Well, the short answer is, *I don't know*. I can tell you that exhaustion is still a nagging issue since falling asleep still makes me think about not waking up, and once I *am* asleep, my unresolved sleep apnea leaves me unable to get that ever-elusive *deep sleep*. Besides the sleep troubles, I could share how disappointed I was when I found out I didn't get that job I was hoping for, even though I'm sure they had good reasons for hiring someone else. But on a more positive note, I could share how most of the adjustment challenges that I mentioned earlier have eased: I have a well-established routine now for taking my meds, the equilibrium issues have mostly leveled off, and my headaches are pretty much under control. Plus, having just passed the six-month point, many of those "firsts" I talked about are out of the way.

I am still eating healthy and exercising. I'm taking my meds faithfully and seeing both my primary care doctor and Dr. Mayuga regularly. I'm also very committed to continuing with counseling to bring healing to my mind. And yes, I still pray when I hear an ambulance drive by.

If you actually want a couple more updates, I could share how, after not having to go to the Emergency Room for almost four months, I had to go back twice in the past six weeks: On April 28th, I drove myself to the hospital because I had blood in my urine for the first time. (Gross, I know.) I was encouraged to go to the ER by both my primary care doctor and my cardiologist because the possibility of a UTI (Urinary Tract Infection) was a concern. But I'm happy to report that after a CAT scan and some blood tests, I was told I did *not* have an infection and it was just a temporary side effect of being on blood-altering meds. Then, on June 3rd, after kayaking with Molly and her dad for a couple hours that morning, I began having chest pains around 9:00 PM. Each time I inhaled, I felt sharp pain directly over my heart. Under advisement from a paramedic friend, Molly and I drove to the fire station. After being looked at by the paramedics there, I took another ambulance ride to the ER. I suspected the pain might just be the result of muscle strain from kayaking, but if I'm learning anything through this, it's that *guessing* about these things is a fool's errand. Even though I was in very capable hands both in the ambulance and at the hospital, I found myself with a strong awareness of my mortality once again. As we waited for EKG and bloodwork results, I tried to not worry. Fortunately, my EKG results and troponin levels were normal, so this too was most likely not a heart-related incident. Well, I think these updates have been more than enough for you to read. Besides, if I share any more, this "little book" won't be so *little* after all.

The latest research indicates that people who suffer cardiac arrest have a 15% chance of recurrence, typically occurring in the first year. No, that percentage isn't very high, though I'll admit it was kind of discouraging when I first heard it. But when I guess as to the number of people comprising that statistic who made no significant changes to their lifestyle, I suspect the odds of recurrence may be even less for me because I'm at least giving it some real effort. But at the end of the day, "15%" is a statistic and not a certainty anyway. Besides, what choice do I have? Give up? That's not an option that I have any right to entertain. There's too much to live for.

I'm going to live what life I have left with *purpose*. I'm going to live it with *gratitude*. And I'm going to live it with *respect* for just how brief and fragile life can be. I'm pretty sure someone once likened this life to a *mist* or a *vapor* that appears for a little while and then vanishes. We are never guaranteed even the next moment, let alone years to come, and I can tell you, now more than ever, that is something I firmly believe. The only furtherance of my life that I can point to with certainty, is the additional six months—and counting—that I've already been given.

At first, this whole situation made me think about racking up as many exciting, "bucket list" experiences as I could before knocking on death's door again. I quickly realized I didn't really want that. I'd prefer instead to continue doing the things I knew mattered *before* all of this happened. I want to live out what is perhaps most succinctly found in the message of Micah: *to do what's right, to embrace mercy, and to walk humbly with God.* Living this way is so much more important than racking up personal experiences to merely enrich myself or impress others.

There will be a day that I die again, and not temporarily like last time. On *that* day, I'll go trusting in the reality of Jesus' historical resurrection. Because He triumphed over death, I have assurance that I will know life beyond the grave as well. We all know that death follows life. We see *that* every day. But I also have hope that life can follow death, much like the way a seed that is sown waits for a new reality that it cannot comprehend.

Let me end this book by focusing on the fact that, though told through my eyes, this whole experience has never really been about *me*. Even the deeply personal encounter with clinical death that I shared about, wasn't *just* personal. All of the men and women that I wrote about—who made such an incredible difference in saving my life—*they* were the ones I see standing on center stage that day. And the path I've walked in the six months since then wasn't traveled alone either. So many friends, family, and even strangers came alongside to care for us and are central to those parts of the story as well.

But I'm convinced there's no way I could fully explain to you the many ways in which Molly has been my most meaningful friend on this journey. She is my *"one true companion"* as our song says. For 27 years she has been by my side through thick and thin. (And I'm not just talking about my weight.) It wouldn't be an exaggeration to say that she has been absolutely *essential* to my very survival.

One morning recently, Molly noticed that I was, for the thousandth time, rubbing my chest as I tried to guess if the sensation I was feeling was something serious. Concerned, she asked me, "How's your heart?" I was pretty sure that the sensation was nothing to worry about again this time, but as I lay there a few moments, I reflected on what we had come through. I immediately saw in my mind's eye many of the ways we had been the recipients of such selfless kindness from so many people. "What a question," I thought. ... *"How's my heart?"*

I just smiled at Molly and told her, "It's full."

PHOTO ALBUM: PROGRESS

October 15, 2022

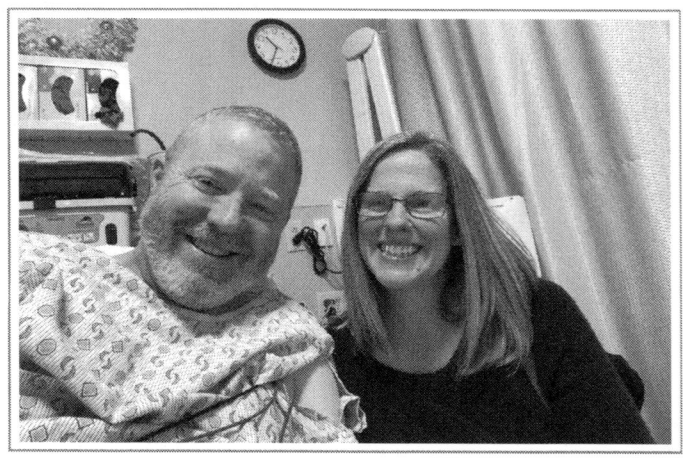

December 21, 2022

April 16, 2023

May 21, 2023

*WHAT I NEED TO DO TO ADDRESS
MY OWN HEART HEALTH:*

SPECIAL THANKS

To those of you who graciously provided me with your feedback ahead of publication—Molly, Vera, Kathi, Marcia, Dane, Trish, Ami, Ryan, Haylee, Sara, Joseph, Andrew, Kaylie, and Clete—thank you all so much!